STREET SCENES
AND
ARCHITECTURE

A Colouring Book for Grown-ups

All you need:

- Colouring Pens or Pencils
- A bit of imagination

Tip: Use darker colours on the darker shaded areas and lighter colours for the light shaded areas

Eduardo hopes that you will have as much fun colouring this book as he had creating it!

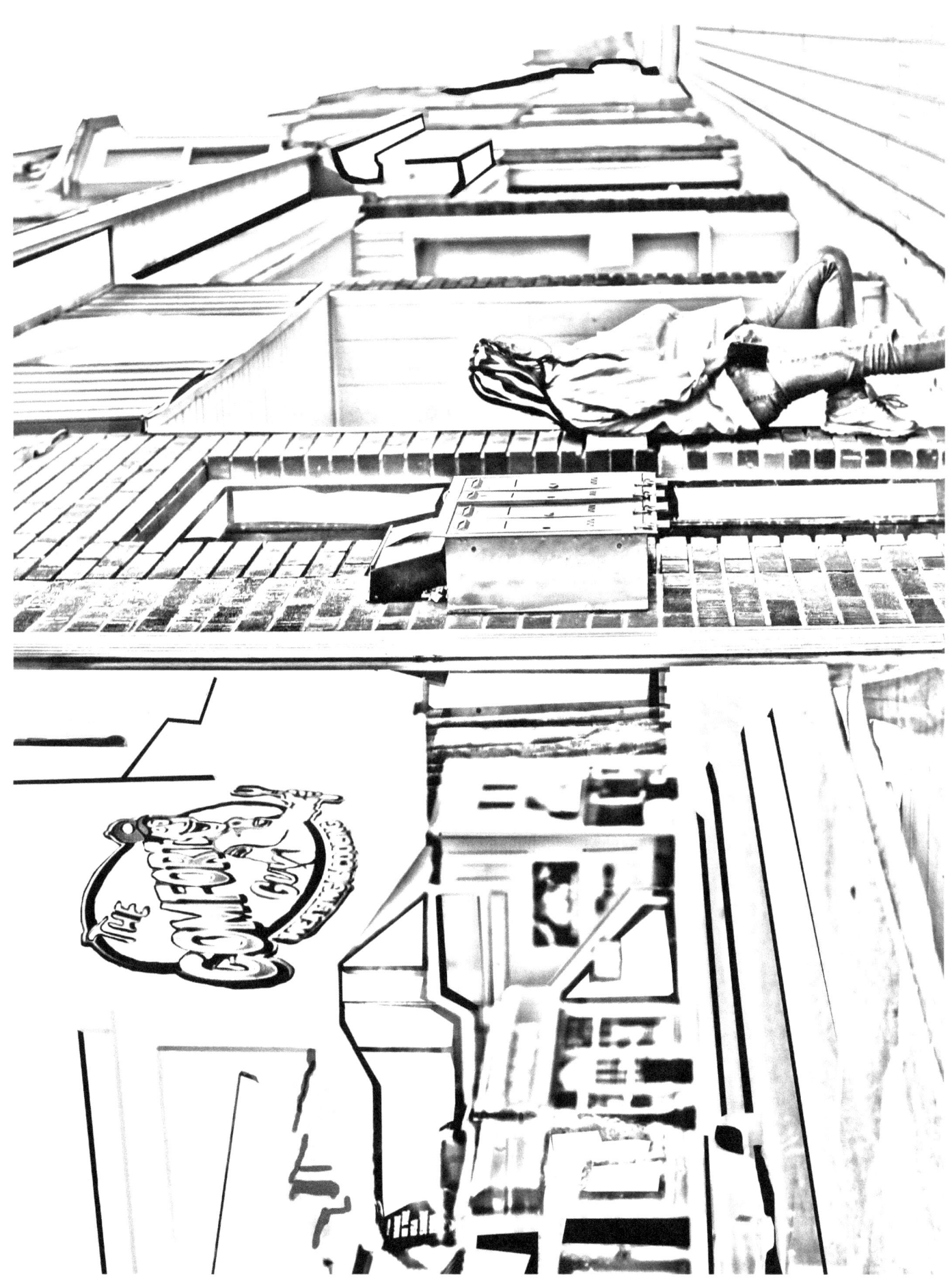

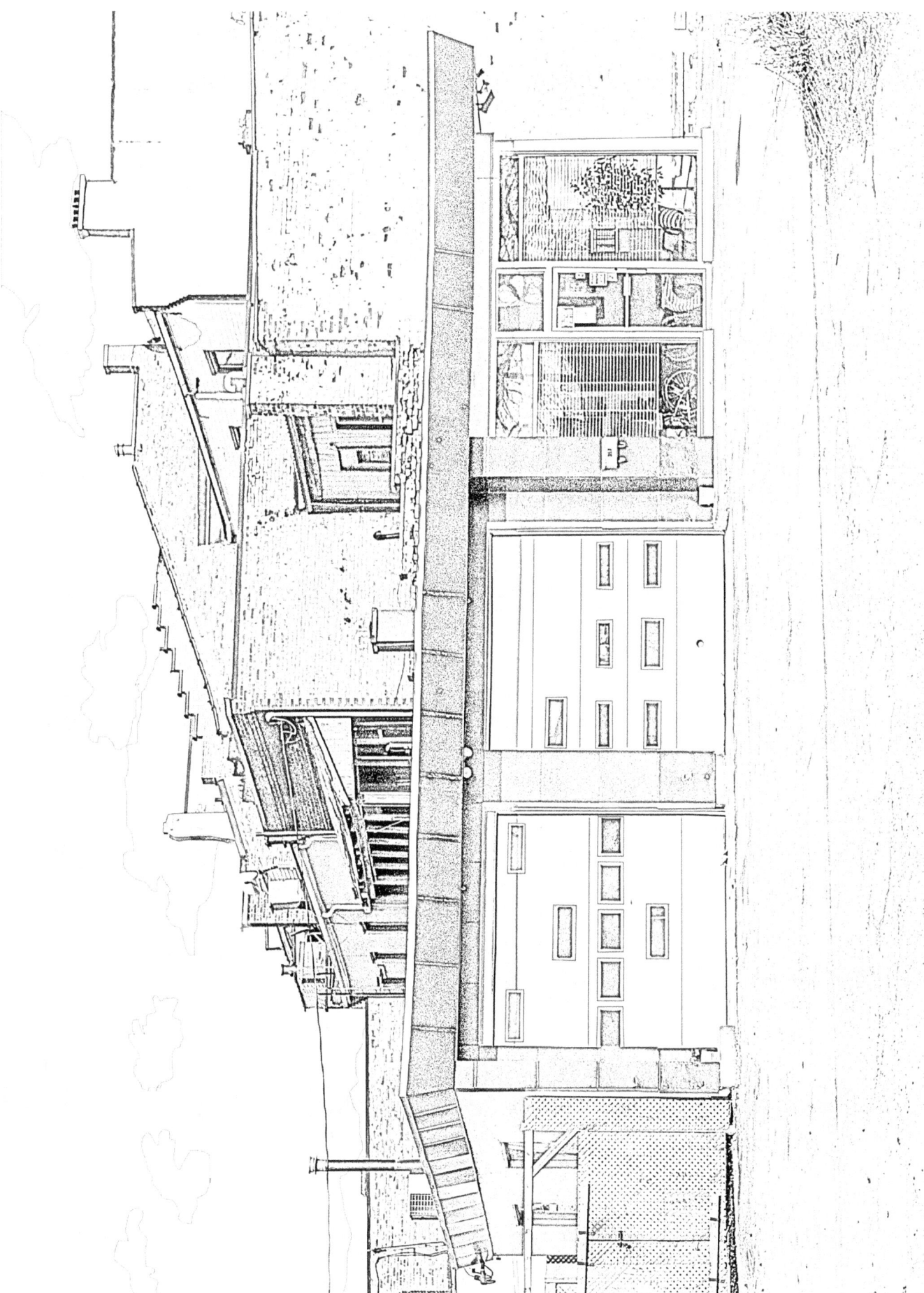

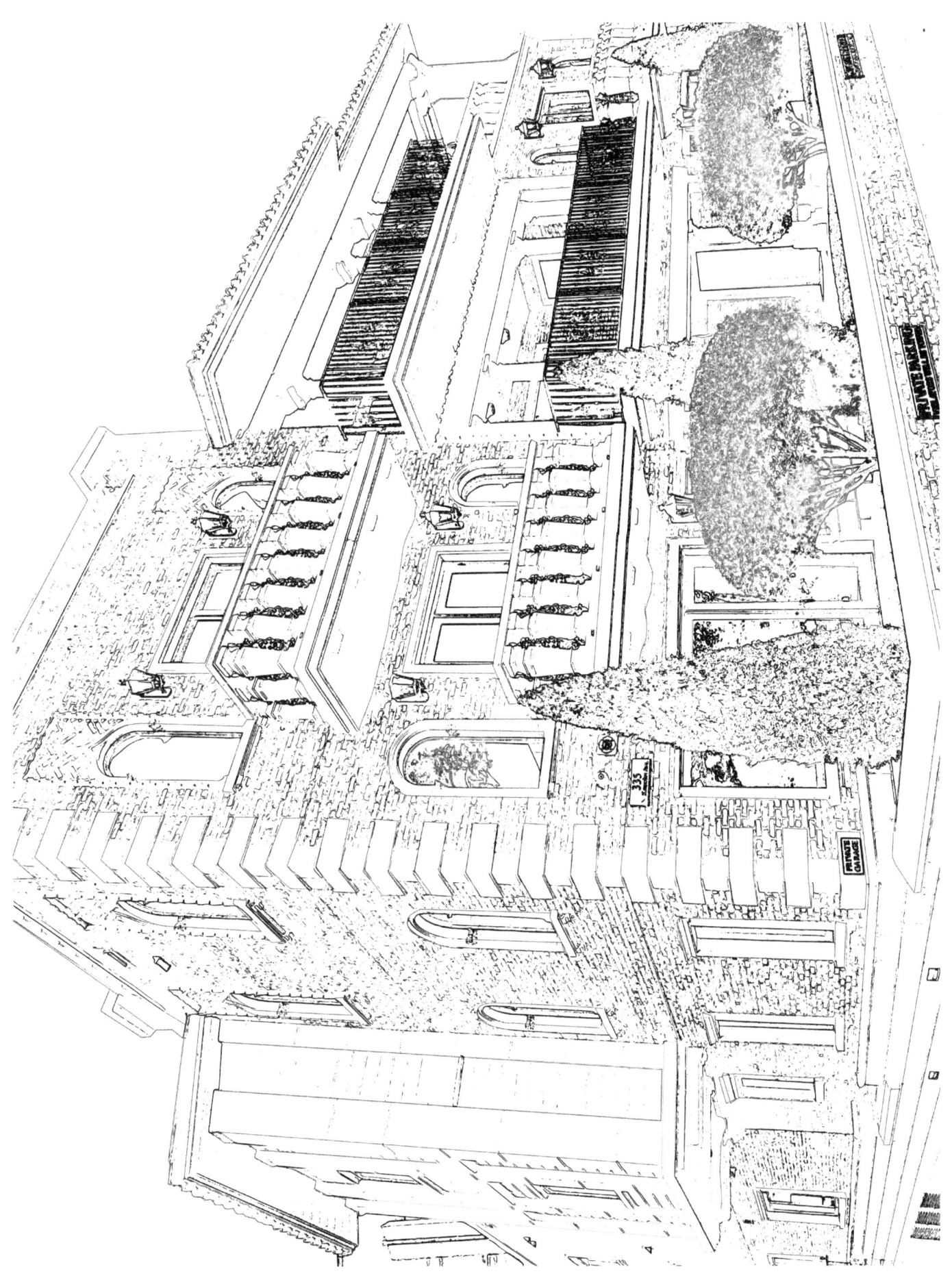

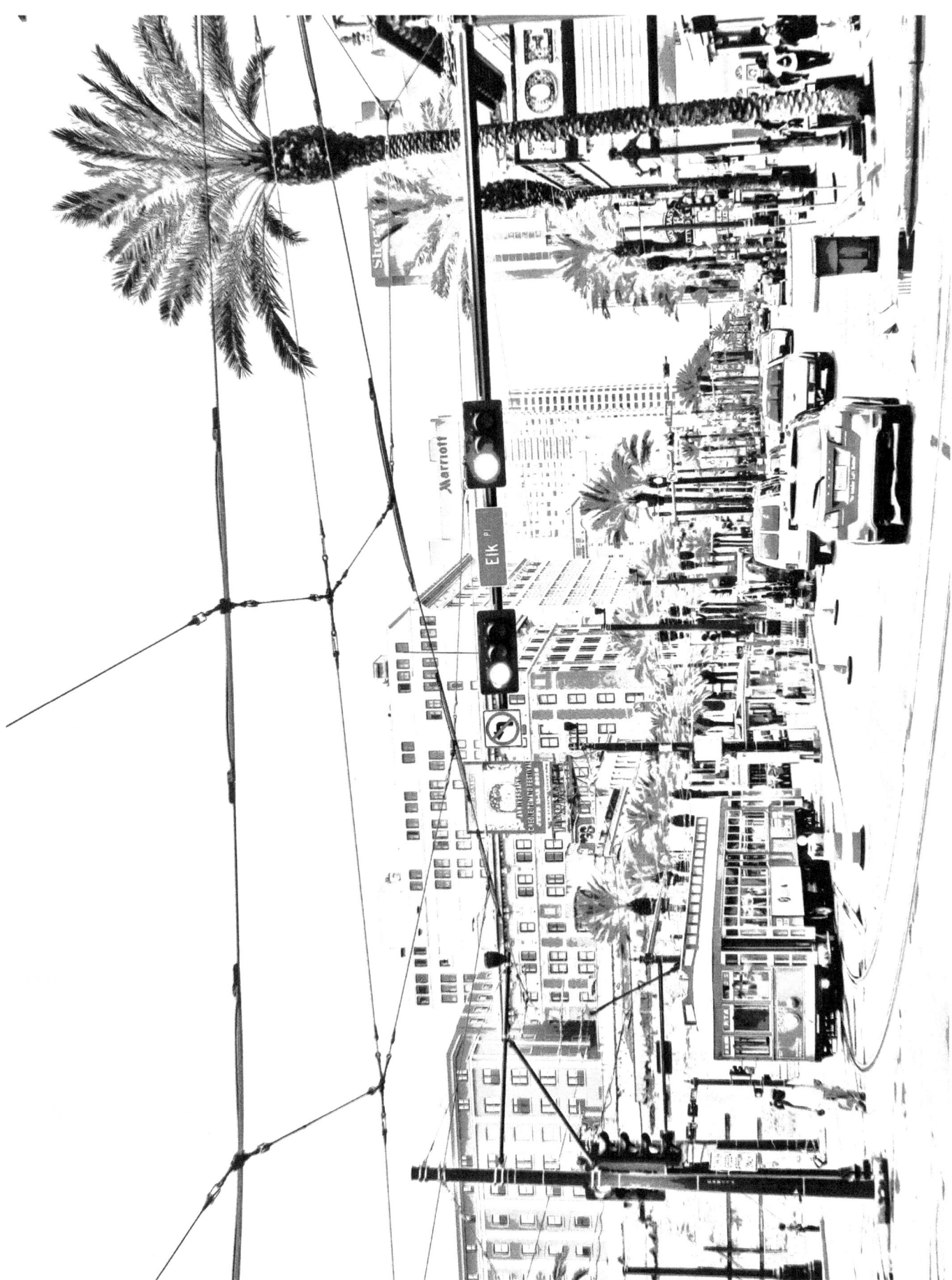

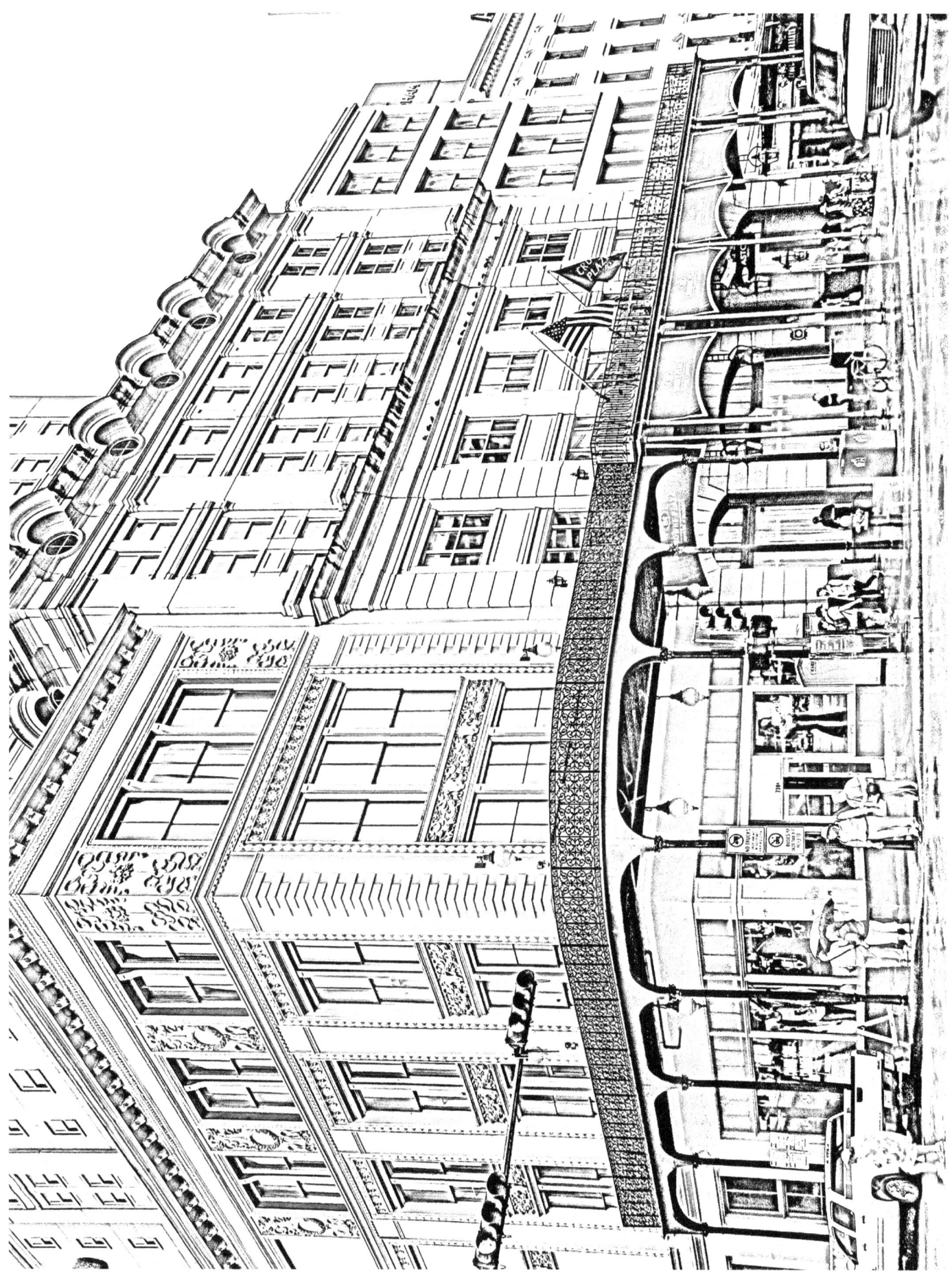

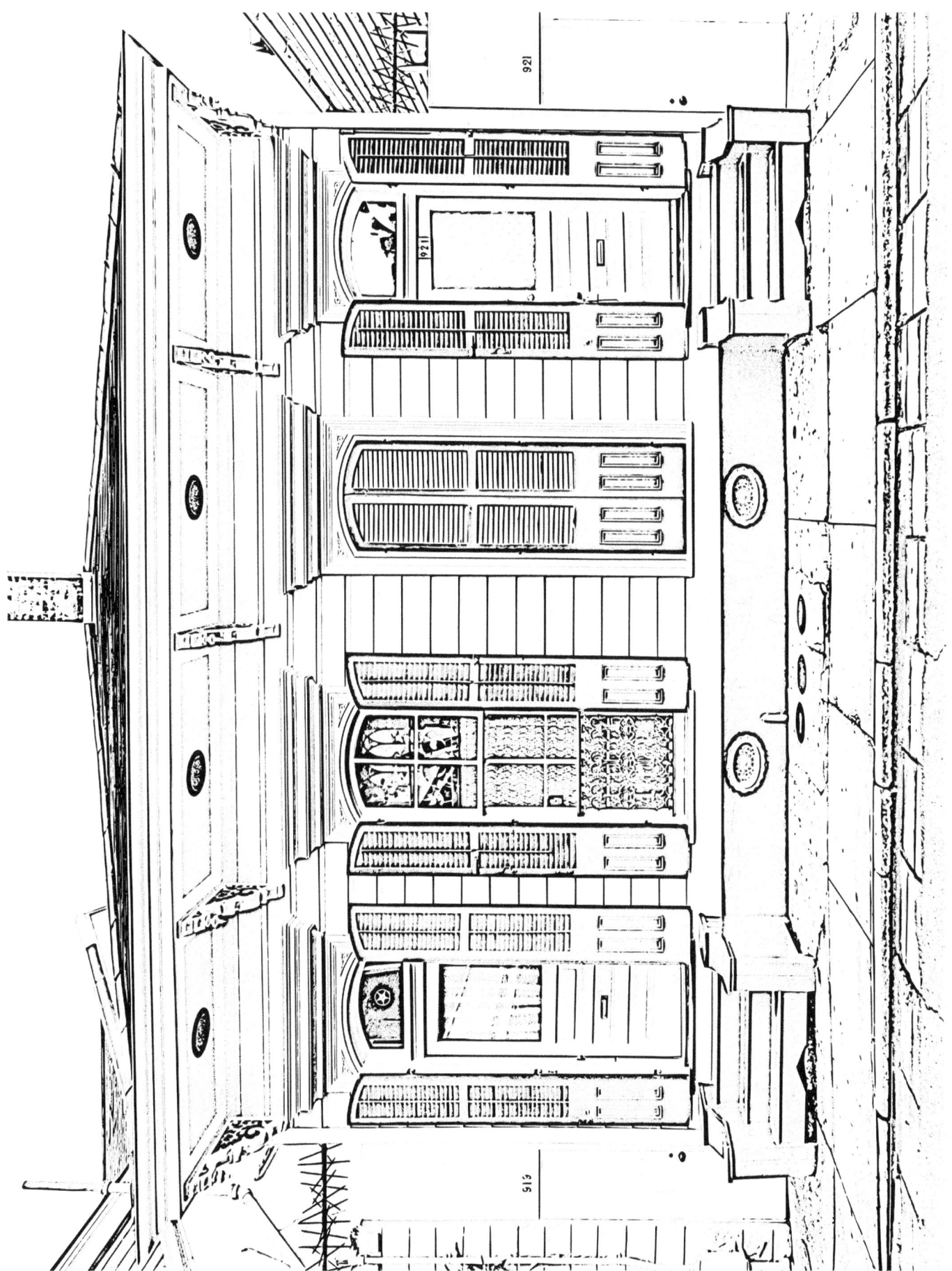

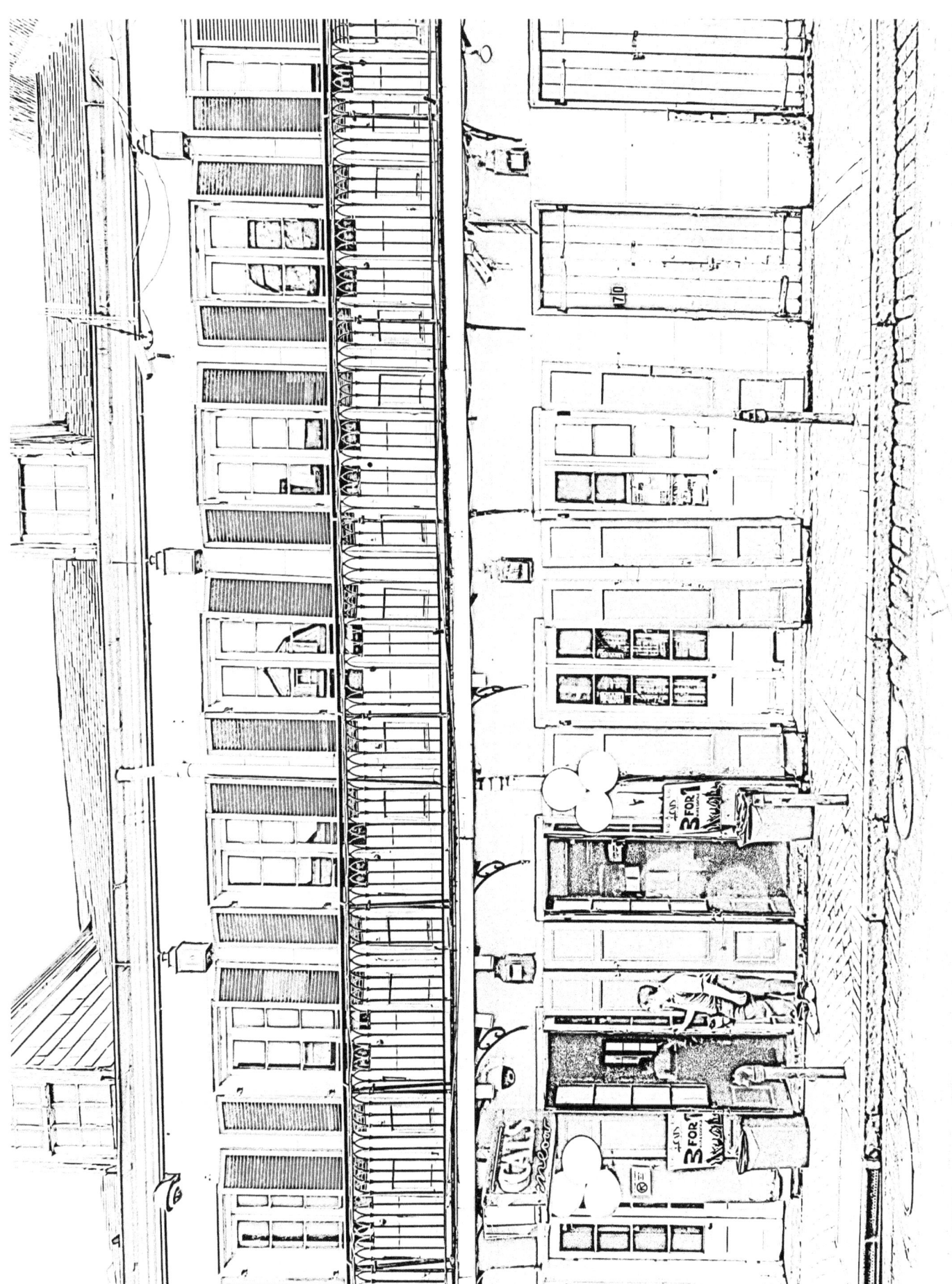

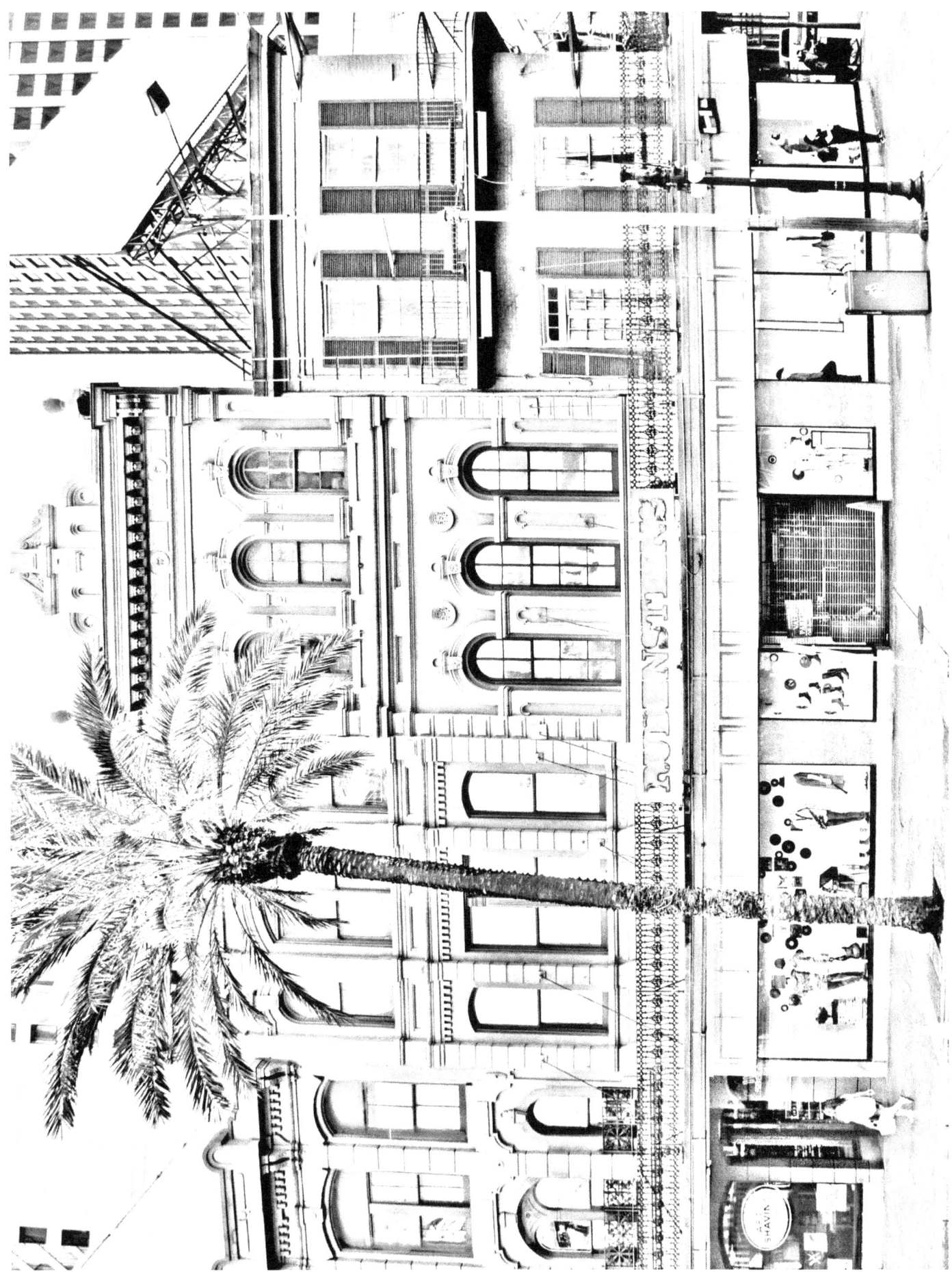

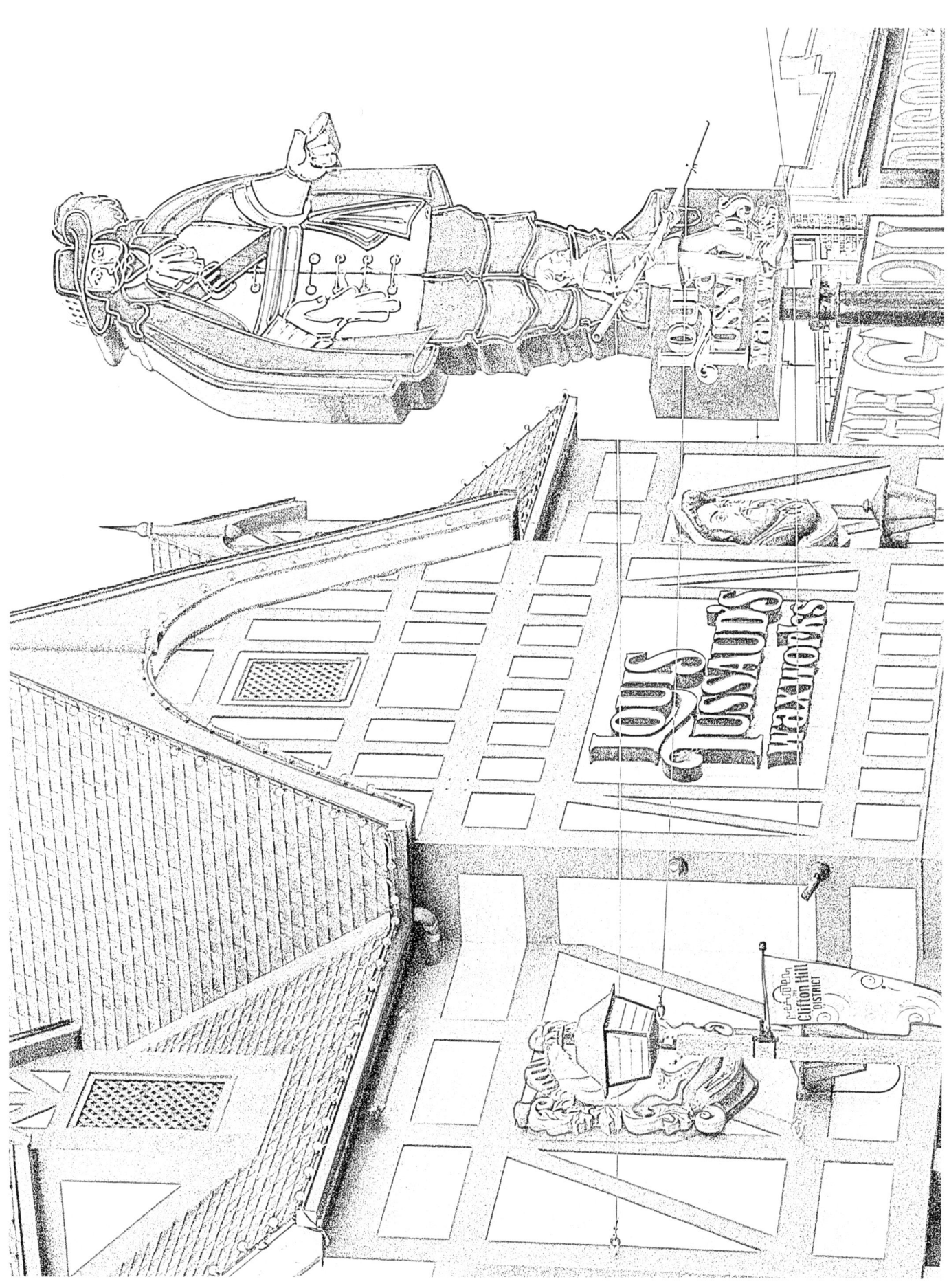